Teaching Tradition of Advaita Vedanta

Swami Dayananda Saraswati
Arsha Vidya

Arsha Vidya
Research and Publication Trust
Chennai

Published by :

Arsha Vidya Research
and Publication Trust
4 'Sri Nidhi' Apts 3rd Floor
Sir Desika Road Mylapore
Chennai 600 004 INDIA
Tel : 044 2499 7023
Telefax : 2499 7131
Email : avrandpt@gmail.com
Website : avrpt.com

ISBN : 978-81-906059-4-6

Revised Edition	:	May 2009	Copies :	2000
1st Reprint	:	June 2011	Copies :	1000
2nd Reprint	:	July 2013	Copies :	1000

Design & format :
Graaphic Design

Printed at :
Sudarsan Graphics
27, Neelakanta Mehta Street
T. Nagar, Chennai 600 017
Email : info@sudarsan.com

Contents

Key to Transliteration and Pronunciation of Sanskrit Letters

Sanskrit is a highly phonetic language and hence accuracy in articulation of the letters is important. For those unfamiliar with the *Devanāgari* script, the international transliteration is a guide to the proper pronunciation of Sanskrit letters.

अ	*a*	*(but)*
आ	*ā*	*(father)*
इ	*i*	*(it)*
ई	*ī*	*(beat)*
उ	*u*	*(full)*
ऊ	*ū*	*(pool)*
ऋ	*ṛ*	*(rhythm)*
ॠ	*ṝ*	*(marine)*
ऌ	*ḷ*	*(revelry)*
ए	*e*	*(play)*
ऐ	*ai*	*(aisle)*
ओ	*o*	*(go)*
औ	*au*	*(loud)*
क	*ka*	*(seek)* 1
ख	*kha*	*(blockhead)**1
ग	*ga*	*(get)* 1
घ	*gha*	*(log hut)**1
ङ	*ṅa*	*(sing)* 1
च	*ca*	*(chunk)* 2
छ	*cha*	*(catch him)**2
ज	*ja*	*(jump)* 2
झ	*jha*	*(hedgehog)**2
ञ	*ña*	*(bunch)* 2
ट	*ṭa*	*(true)**3
ठ	*ṭha*	*(anthill)**3
ड	*ḍa*	*(drum)**3
ढ	*ḍha*	*(godhead)**3
ण	*ṇa*	*(under)**3
त	*ta*	*(path)**4
थ	*tha*	*(thunder)**4
द	*da*	*(that)**4
ध	*dha*	*(breathe)**4
न	*na*	*(nut)**4
प	*pa*	*(put)* 5
फ	*pha*	*(loophole)**5
ब	*ba*	*(bin)* 5
भ	*bha*	*(abhor)**5
म	*ma*	*(much)* 5
य	*ya*	*(loyal)*
र	*ra*	*(red)*
ल	*la*	*(luck)*
व	*va*	*(vase)*
श	*śa*	*(sure)*
ष	*ṣa*	*(shun)*
स	*sa*	*(so)*
ह	*ha*	*(hum)*

•	*ṁ*	*anusvāra*	(nasalisation of preceding vowel)
:	*ḥ*	*visarga*	(aspiration of preceding vowel)
*			No exact English equivalents for these letters

1.	Guttural	–	Pronounced from throat
2.	Palatal	–	Pronounced from palate
3.	Lingual	–	Pronounced from cerebrum
4.	Dental	–	Pronounced from teeth
5.	Labial	–	Pronounced from lips

The 5th letter of each of the above class – called nasals – are also pronounced nasally.

Preface

Advaita Vedanta is a teaching tradition. When one receives the teaching from a traditional teacher, one also comes to know the whole method of teaching. In the teaching itself is the method discussed. Exposure to a wrong method makes one miss the vision of the teaching. Therefore, in this book what is not the teaching, including its methodology, is discussed. Some of the modern concepts are also examined in this small book. So, I recommend this book to every student of Vedanta for serious study.

Swami Dayananda Saraswati
April 27 2009
Coimbatore

Introduction

I call myself a traditional teacher of Vedanta. Teacher of Vedanta should be enough. Why this adjective 'traditional'? I am constrained to use this word for a number of reasons. Many modern academicians as well as several Hindu spiritual teachers present Advaita Vedanta as a school of thought, promising an experience of oneness of the individual soul, *jīva*, with the Lord, Īśvara. For this promised experience, certain practices are prescribed which vary from teacher to teacher. In this brief presentation I attempt to analyse some of these contentions more to help one see what is traditional Vedanta than to criticise any given person.

Advaita Vedanta

The subject matter of Vedanta is the most desirable, *hita*, for every individual. Analysing the various ends, *puruṣārthas*, in life such as security-*artha*; pleasure-*kāma*; and *dharma* that is *puṇya*, for the hereafter, Vedanta presents *mokṣa*, freedom from limitation, as the most desirable.

Analysing these *puruṣārthas*, the *Muṇḍakopaniṣad* says,[1] 'the uncreated is not created by an action.'

Kṛta means what is made or created. *Akṛta* means what is not created, something real, the *vastu,* which exists without being created. The same *vastu* is presented in other *upaniṣad*s as *satya*. The *Chāndogyopaniṣad* says, "Before creation, this world existed only as *sat*."[2] Since *sat* existed before the creation of the world, which includes time, it is outside the scope of time and therefore timeless, eternal. Being already existent, *sat* is not produced by any action performed. The self, *ātman* is equated to this *satya* and therefore, you are *satya.*

Knowledge of this *satya* as oneself is the most desirable *puruṣārtha*. In fact, it is the only real end in life, *parama-puruṣārtha*. The *Chāndogyopaniṣad* also presents the same knowledge as freedom from sorrow now, and from the cycle of *saṁsāra,* a life of becoming, forever. Self-knowledge being the solution to the problem of sorrow, the subject matter unfolded by the *upaniṣad*s, naturally, becomes the most desirable end for a human being. Therefore, the *Muṇḍakopaniṣad* advises the seeker to go to a teacher who is well-versed in the *śāstra* in order to gain self-knowledge.[3]

Is Vedanta a school of thought?

A school of thought is always propounded by a given person or persons. A school of thought, being what it is, is subject to dispute. The propounder's means of knowledge, such as perception and inference, should find access to the subject matter that he or she propounds. The subject matter of Vedanta is not available for the propounder's means of knowledge. If it is, then who is the subject who employs the means of knowledge? Suppose I am the subject. How can I be the object about which I have a contention? So the subject matter of Vedanta, which is *ātman*, can never be a school of thought.

Any thought regarding the *ātman* is a speculation. The *upaniṣad*s themselves make this clear. "Understand that to be Brahman, *ātman*, which is not objectified by the mind and because of which the mind knows everything."[4] Analysing the subject matter of Vedanta in the light of various schools of thought prevalent in his time, Vyāsa presents Vedanta as a means of knowledge, *pramāṇa*, for knowing *brahmātman*, the self being Brahman.[5] Therefore, to consider Vedanta as another school of thought, along with other schools of thought including the mechanical materialists, *Cārvāka*s, and so on, is not reasonable.

There are many books in circulation that discuss the six schools of Indian philosophy, and Vedanta is also included as one among them. This inclusion is not justified because, unlike a school of thought, Vedanta is not within the realm of speculation. The subject matter of the entire Veda is *pramāṇāntara-anadhigatam,* one that various means of knowledge such as perception and inference have no access to. There is no way to prove or disprove the existence of *puṇya* and *pāpa*. So too, one has no epistemological access to areas such as heaven, rebirth, the structure of a ritual and its connection to its end. These areas fall outside the usual means of knowledge and, therefore, are not subject to any contention.

From the nature of its subject matter, the Veda has to be looked upon as an independent means of knowledge, *svataḥ-pramāṇam*. The *upaniṣad*s, forming the last portion of the Veda, also have a subject matter which is not available for sensory perception and inference. Therefore, to label Vedanta as a school of thought stems from misunderstanding regarding the nature of its subject matter.

There are teachers, *ācārya*s, who interpret the sentences of Vedanta, *vedānta-vākya*s, differently; but all these *ācārya*s look upon Vedanta as a *pramāṇa*. How valid are their interpretations? The answer to this question will lead to an analysis, *mīmāṁsā*, of the sentences of the various *upaniṣads* constituting Vedanta. In this analysis, we employ reasoning, *yukti*, grammar, *vyākaraṇa*, and other factors that constitute hermeneutics. By such inquiry, *vicāra*, the vision, *tātparya*, of Vedanta will become clear. Therefore, the interpretations of Rāmānuja, Mādhva,Vallabha and others who accept Vedanta as a means of knowledge cannot be considered schools of thought, but only as interpretations of Vedanta.

If Vedanta is a *pramāṇa*, then viewing it as such is called *śraddhā*, trust in the validity of Vedanta, pending knowledge. To verify a means of knowledge, you do not require another means of knowledge, it rests in itself. To know that your eyes see, you have to use your eyes and see. To know that Vedanta is a means of knowledge you have to expose yourself dispassionately to Vedanta with *śraddhā*, and see whether what it unfolds is true. If what Vedanta says is contradicted by any other means of knowledge, then the whole subject matter of Vedanta has to be dismissed as not valid, or it has to be looked into again. You cannot say, "Because I see this man, he does not talk." Seeing does not contradict hearing. Similarly, your perception or inference about various things in the world does not, in any way, contradict the vision unfolded by Vedanta.

The vision and teaching methods in Vedanta

The vision of Vedanta is an equation of the identity between the *jīva,* individual, and Īśvara, the Lord. This vision of oneness, *aikya,* is not available for perception or inference. Nor is the oneness that is unfolded by Vedanta contradicted by perception or inference. Oneness is purely in terms of understanding the equation. Vedanta does not promise a salvation to the soul. In its vision, the soul, the *ātman,* is already free from any limitation. Freedom from limitation is a fact and the release of the individual from this sense of limitation is the outcome of understanding the equation. Therefore, the entire teaching of Vedanta can be expressed in one sentence—*tat tvam asi,* that thou art. All other sentences in the *upaniṣad*s are only meant to prove this equation.

The proofs consist of a number of methods, *prakriyā*s, adopted by the *upaniṣad*s, and by the teachers in the tradition, to communicate the vision of the *mahāvākya, tat tvam asi,* the sentence revealing the oneness of the individual and the Lord. To unfold this identity between the *jīva* and Īśvara, Vedanta employs these *prakriyā*s. If a system of philosophy is formulated based on these *prakriyās*, the whole purpose of Vedanta, which is to reveal the reality, *vastu*, is defeated. Therefore, Vedanta is a *pramāṇa* only to reveal the oneness of *ātman*, the self, with Īśvara.

Vedanta is not a *pramāṇa* to prove the existence of *atman*, for the only self-existent, self-evident thing in this world is oneself, *ātman*. The whole world, *kṣetra*, including my physical body, mind and senses becomes evident to me, the knower, *kṣetrajña*. The *kṣetrajña* is self-revealing and therefore self-evident, while everything else becomes evident to the self. Any evidence is in terms of knowledge. Any knowledge implies the presence of consciousness. The invariable factor in all forms of knowledge is but this consciousness.

Kāraṇa-kārya-prakriyā

One of the main *prakriyās* is *kāraṇa-kārya vāda*. Brahman is presented in the *upaniṣads* as the cause of everything: "From which all these elements have come, by which all these are sustained and unto which all these go back, understand that to be Brahman."[6] Further, Brahman the cause of the world is *satya*. The *jagat* presented in the *śruti* in the form of five basic subtle and gross elements, is the effect, *kārya*, of *satya*, the *kāraṇa*.

Jagat being an effect, *kārya*, is *mithyā* as revealed by the famous *vācārambhana-śruti*.[7] The *śruti* presents the *kārya* as neither *satya*, that which exists; nor *tuccha*, that which does not exist; but as *mithyā*, that which has a dependent existence. The *jīva*'s physical body, mind and senses are all within the *kārya* and are, therefore, *mithyā*, but the *jīva* is not created and its nature, *svarūpa*, is *satyam jñānam anantaṁ*, the limitless consciousness that is the reality of everything.

If a product, *kārya*, is non-separate from the *kāraṇa*, the material cause, then the cause and effect are not two separate things. The effect is not separate from the cause and the cause, being what it is, is independent of the effect. The *Chandogyopaniṣad*, therefore, makes an opening statement, *pratijña*, that knowing one thing everything would as well be known. This *pratijña* is established by proving that the *kārya* is non-separate from the *kāraṇa*. Therefore, the *kārya* is essentially the *kāraṇa*. A clay pot is but clay. If there is more than one pot, then also it is clay. The plurality of the *kārya* does not make any addition to the clay. If the elemental *jagat* which includes my physical body, *prāṇa* senses and mind is from one non-dual Brahman, then that *jagat*, being an effect, is non-separate from the cause, Brahman. Brahman is the uncreated *tvam*, you, the self, which is *satyam-jñānam-anantaṁ*. The recognition of this fact that I am that *satyam brahma* and that this *jagat* is non-separate from me, while I am independent of the *jagat*, is the result of the teaching of Vedanta. That recognition of oneself as *sarvātman*, as the whole, is the ultimate end, called *mokṣa*. The *upaniṣads*, praising the one who has the knowledge of oneself as everything, say, 'that one crosses sorrow.'[8] The *upaniṣads* rightly say that there is no *saṁsāra* for the person because he or she is free from all sense of limitations.

Avasthā-traya-prakriyā

Another important *prakriyā* employed in the *upaniṣads* is an analysis of the three states of experience, waking, dream and sleep. In this analysis the *śāstra* employs *anvaya-vyatireka* reasoning[9] to arrive at the true nature of oneself. The waker and the waking world are absent in both dream and sleep. The dreamer and the dream world are absent in both waking and sleep. In sleep the status of the dreamer and the waker is absent.

If the status of the subject is real, one cannot give up this status at any time. What is intrinsic to an object should be present in the object as long as the object exists. If it is not present, then it is an incidental attribute.

An example often cited in this context is the crystal assuming a colour in the presence of a coloured object. If the colour is intrinsic to the crystal, it will be present therein as long as the crystal exists. But when the coloured object is taken away, the colour, which was seen in the crystal, disappears. Therefore, the colour assumed by the crystal is incidental, *upādhi kṛtā*. In the sleep experience, and also in the waking state where there is absence of the subject-object relationship, there is no status for oneself as the subject. Hence, the subject-object status must be assumed to be incidental. Analysing these experiences, the *śāstra* presents the *ātman* as free from all attributes imputed to it.

Any attribute is purely incidental, and not intrinsic. If *ātman* is attribute-free, is it non-existent, *śūnya*? No, because the concept of *śūnya* itself is a piece of knowledge implying a subject, a knower. The *śāstra* describes the *ātman* as *jyotiḥ, jñānam, sākṣī, cetā* and so on. All these words mean the content of the subject, the knower, which we may call consciousness.

Consciousness is invariable in all the states of experience while consciousness itself is free from any attribute. Therefore, when the *śāstra* uses the word attribute-free *ātman, nirviśeṣa ātman*, it means the *svarūpa* of *ātman* as pure consciousness. All attributes such as doership and enjoyership are purely incidental. *Ācārya* Gauḍapāda and others who came later deftly handle this *prakriyā* presented in the *Māṇḍūkyopaniṣad* to unfold the fact that the self is Brahman, and the world, implying the subject-object relationship, is purely an incidental attribute of Brahman and is, therefore, *mithyā*.

Pañca-kośa-prakriyā

Another well-known *prakriyā* is the analysis of the *pañca-kośa*. In the *Taittirīyopaniṣad* we see this *prakriyā*. *Kośa* means a cover, a sheath. The five *kośa*s are presented as the covers for *ātman*. If *ātman* is invariable in all the situations, there cannot be any cover for the *ātman*. So how can there be covers? We have to understand that they are only seeming covers—*kośavat ācchādakatvāt kośaḥ*. Born of self-ignorance, there are five universal erroneous notions. The cause, *nimitta*, for each notion is said to be a *kośa*. The physical body, *anna-maya*, is one *kośa* inasmuch as it is taken to be oneself. I am mortal, I am tall, I am male, I am female, all these notions are imputed to *ātman*, with reference to the physical body. This being universal, the physical body becomes a *kośa*. So too, when one says, 'I am hungry, I am thirsty,' *ātman* is taken to be subject to hunger and thirst and *prāṇa-maya* becomes a *kośa*.

The notions that I am sad, I am agitated, are due to *mano-maya kośa*. The *vijñāna-maya* is also a *kośa* because the sense of doer-ship, which is its attribute, is taken to belong to *ātman* and the notion, 'I am the doer' is the outcome. *Ānanda-maya* is a *kośa*, with reference to enjoyership, in the form of degrees of experienced happiness. While the presence of *ātman* is there in all the five *kośa*s, *ātman* itself is free from all of them.

A teacher has to show that while the *kośas* are *ātman*, *ātman* is always free from the *kośa*s, being uninvolved, *asaṅga*. *Ātman* is to be unfolded following the *sthūlārundhatī-nyāya*.[10] The *Taittirīyopaniṣad* presents this method by first introducing *anna-maya*, which is *sthūla deha*, the gross physical body, as *ātman*.[11] Then by saying that there is another *ātman*, it negates the previous notion. The process continues until the *ātman* as Brahman is pointed out as the basis of *ānanda-maya*. Here, the *ātman* is not to be taken as something hidden, as it is frequently interpreted in modern Vedanta, where the *kośa*s are considered to cover the *ātman*. Modern Vedanta talks about some kind of transcendental experience obtaining beyond all these *kośa*s. This is a typical example of how a *prakriyā* is taken as a system and the subsequent inconsistencies are left unexplained.

Sarvātma-bhāva

As I have briefly shown, the *prakriyā*s adopted by the *upaniṣad*s are meant to reveal the truth of the self being attribute-free, limitless Brahman. Since *brahma-ātman* does not undergo any change, whatsoever, the *kāraṇa-kārya prakriyā* is only meant to unfold the fact that the self is limitless and the world is non-separate from it. The vision of Vedanta is not so much in presenting a cause-effect relationship between Brahman and the *jagat* as it is in unfolding the *jagat* as non-separate from Brahman. This *sarvātma bhāva*, recognition of oneself as the whole, is the vision, *tātparya*, of the *śruti*.

The *avasthā-traya-prakriyā* is not for presenting a fourth state of experience, but only to point out that the invariable consciousness in all three states is Brahman, the *adhiṣṭhāna*, and the truth of the entire world. The *pañca-kośa prakriyā* does not present a hidden *ātman* but only points out the universal mistake committed at each of the five levels of experience. The attributes of *kāraṇa*, *avasthā*, *kośa* and others, initially mentioned for Brahman, are later negated in the *prakriyā*s. By this negation, *apavāda*, the attributes are seen as only a superimposition, *adhyāropa*, on Brahman. This method is called *adhyāropa-*

apavāda nyāya. The way in which the *prakriyā*s are handled utilising the method of *adhyāropa-apavāda* is important to understand. If Vedanta is presented as a system of philosophy, there is no handling involved; what counts is only a clear presentation of the system. If the vision of *sarvātma-bhāva* is to be unfolded, it is altogether different.

The role of guru in resolving confusions

A *guru* is important in gaining self-knowledge because the handling of *prakriyās* is involved in unfolding the truth. If one does not handle the *prakriyās* as they should be, one can only tell one's disciples that Vedanta is a theory, that practice gives the experience of the self. But when Vedanta is a means of knowledge, it is neither theory nor practice that will bring an experience of the self. The self, which is the content of all experiences, is consciousness by nature, *anubhūti svarūpa*, and it does not become an object of experience, implying another hypothetical subject besides the self.

The failure to understand the subject matter and the nature of the *prakriyās* adopted by the *śāstra* have given rise to a number of confusions in the minds of both seekers and masters. Let us analyse some of the areas of confusion here:

Ātman-bliss confusion

Brahma-ātman is presented in the *śāstra* as *ānanda*. This one experiential word '*ānanda*' is frequently a cause for confusion. The *Taittirīyopaniṣad* presents Brahman as *satyam jñānam anantaṁ*. These three words are equivalent to *sat-cit* and *ānanda*. The meaning of the word *ānanda* is *ananta*, limitlessness. The word, '*satya*' which is generally an attribute to a thing existent in time, is in apposition with the word *ananta*. Because of the qualifying word *ananta, satya* is released from the three-fold limitations of space, time and object-status.[12] At the same time, being the cause of everything, *satya* is the truth of everything that is dependent upon it. And *satya* is also *jñāna*, which as a word can mean knower or knowledge or even known. But with the word *ananta*, the limited meaning of *jñāna* is removed and *jñāna*, the invariable consciousness presence in all these three, becomes its meaning. The invariable content of the knower-known-knowledge is consciousness, which is *satya*. This *satyam-jñānam-anantam*, the consciousness, *ātman*, is predicated to Brahman which is the cause of the entire *jagat*. Later in the *Taittirīyopaniṣad* and elsewhere in the *upaniṣads*, the word *ānanda* is used in the place of *ananta*, which is the *svarūpa* of *ātman*.

Here, the word '*ānanda*' can be translated as bliss if *ānanda* is experiential. But when it is a word unfolding the *svarūpa* of *ātman*, its translation can never be bliss. A special bliss experience is not going to announce, 'I am *ātman* bliss,' so that it can be recognised as unlike any other bliss experienced before. Even if there is an experience of bliss, as modern Vedanta promises, the experience is only as good as we interpret it. And the interpretation is again only as good as our knowledge. Self-knowledge requires a means of knowledge for which we have no refuge except the *śruti.* If the *śruti* is presented as theory, the seeker's initial confusion gets confounded.

Then what is the necessity for using the experiential word *ānanda*? The word serves two purposes:

Firstly, it shows that the knowledge of *ātman* is desirable because *ātman* is *ānanda svarūpa*. Secondly, it shows that the source of all forms of *ānanda* is nothing but the limitlessness of *ātman*.

If *ānanda* is translated as bliss instead of limitlessness or fullness, the seeker is led to believe that there is a special bliss hitherto not experienced. In fact, the *śāstra* says that any form of *ānanda,* whether it is born of sensory experience, *viṣayānanda,* or in the wake of some discovery, *vidyānanda* or by disciplines of *yoga, yogānanda,* is nothing but *svarūpānanda*. The word *ānanda,* therefore, is meant to draw the attention of the seeker to oneself as the source of all *ānanda.* It means the seeker is limitlessness, fullness, which is experienced as happiness whenever the mind meets with the required disposition. The recognition of this fact removes the error of seeing myself as unhappy, ignorant and mortal. So the meaning of the words *sat, cit* and *ānanda* is important in helping the seeker recognise the self as free from all attributes.

Knowledge and realisation confusion

Another confusing word used in modern Vedanta is 'realisation,' often replacing the word knowledge. What is the difference between self-knowledge and self-realisation? According to modern Vedanta, self-knowledge is intellectual while self-realisation is experiential, and because of this difference the study of the *śāstra* is meant for self-knowledge while something else will become the means for self-realisation. When the *śruti* is the means of knowledge to recognise the self, which is always present, *nitya-aparokṣa*, how can there be an indirect knowledge of *ātman*, which has to be converted into direct realisation by some unique method?

Śravaṇam, mananam and *nididhyāsanam* are prescribed in the *śruti* only for self-knowledge. The confusion of making a distinction between knowledge and realisation is caused by not recognising the invariable presence, *aparokṣatvam*, of the *ātman* in all situations and by not understanding the *śruti* as the means of knowledge to recognise the *svarūpa* of *ātman*. That is the reason why we often hear that what we gather from the *śruti* is only intellectual knowledge. The adjective, 'intellectual' describing knowledge will be a necessity only when there is nasal or dental knowledge. All forms of knowledge happen in the intellect. There is no such thing as intellectual knowledge. There can be two types of knowledge, direct and indirect knowledge. When the *ātman* is invariably present, the knowledge of *ātman* can only be direct.[13]

Multi-path confusion

Another popular modern *prakriyā* is that self-knowledge, which is *mokṣa*, can be gained in four different ways. Each way is called *yoga*, different from the other three. One is *jñāna-yoga*, the second *karma-yoga*, the third *bhakti-yoga* and the fourth is *haṭha-yoga*. We are told that each *yoga* is meant for a different type of person. Obviously *jñāna-yoga* is meant for the intellectual, while *karma-yoga* is for the extrovert, *bhakti-yoga* is for the emotional and *haṭha-yoga* is for the one who is not any of these three. The absurdity of this *prakriyā* becomes obvious when we inquire into the nature of self-knowledge. Knowledge does not take place without an appropriate means of knowledge and that knowledge is not the result of any action.

The *śāstra* presents two committed life-styles, *niṣṭās*, for *mokṣa*. One is a life of *sannyāsa*, a commitment to the pursuit of self-knowledge to the exclusion of any other *puruṣārtha*. This is *jñāna-yoga*. A *sannyāsī* does not have obligatory duties. The very Veda which enjoins obligatory duties, releases a *sannyāsī* from those duties and lets him pursue knowledge. The other life-style also involves a commitment to the pursuit of knowledge, but along with *karma* as *yoga*. A *karma-yogī* is equally a *mumukṣa*, one who seeks freedom; but he pursues knowledge along with his obligatory duties. Therefore, a *karma-yogī* has obligatory duties whereas a *sannyāsī* does not.

If there is a third person called a *bhakti-yogī*, does he have obligatory duties or not? If so, he is a *karma-yogī*. Is there a *karma-yogī* without *bhakti*? Is there even a *sannyāsī* without *bhakti*? And what does a *bhakti-yogī* do? If he does daily *pūjā*, it is *kāyikaṁ karma*; if he does *kīrtana*, that is *vācikaṁ karma*; if he does meditation invoking the grace of the Lord, then it is *mānasaṁ karma*. In fact, he is only a *karma-yogī*. Similarly, *haṭha-yoga* may be pursued as a discipline by a *sannyāsī* as well as by a *karma-yogī*, or even by one who is not a *mumukṣu*. It is why Lord Kṛṣṇa says in the third chapter of the *Bhagavad Gītā* "*loke'smin dvividhā niṣṭhā*, there are only two committed life-styles for *mokṣa*." One is *jñāna-yoga*, a life of *sannyāsa* and the other is *karma-yoga*. Both, the *sannyāsī* and the *karma-yogī*, pursue knowledge.

One may argue that in the *Gītā* there is a separate chapter entitled, *bhakti-yoga*. How can there be only a two-fold *yoga*? Each chapter of the *Gītā* is given a title based on the predominant topic therein, and each one is called *yoga* with an adjective to distinguish a given chapter from the others. Again by a wrong translation, we have eighteen *yoga*s starting with the *yoga* of Arjuna's sorrow. In fact, the word *yoga* is used here in the sense of topic; anyone who looks into the Sanskrit thesaurus, *amara-kośa,* will find the word *saṅgati,* connection or in connection with, meaning topic, as a synonym for *yoga*. The predominant topic of the first chapter is Arjuna's sorrow; of the second chapter–knowledge; of the third – *karma,* of the fourth – renunciation of action by knowledge; the fifth – renunciation; the sixth–meditation; and so on. The topic of the twelfth chapter is *bhakti*. It is not *bhakti-yoga*. Even if there is a mention of the compound *bhakti-yoga,* it means only *karma-yoga* or *jñāna-yoga* according to the context.

Therefore, Lord Kṛṣṇa's statement that there are only two *niṣṭhā*s is nowhere contradicted in the *Gītā*.

Whether one takes to a life of *sannyāsa* or leads a life of *karma-yoga*, one has to have the required inner maturity in order to gain clarity in this knowledge. Because *sannyāsa* without inner maturity is not advised in the *Gītā*.[14] A life of *karma-yoga* becomes a necessity for gaining that maturity. The problem being ignorance and error, the solution is knowledge alone; in this, there is no choice. If at all there is a choice, it is only in terms of appropriate life-style. The contention that there are many paths to gain *mokṣa* is false. An integral approach involving all four ways is also meaningless because there are not four approaches in the first place to be integrated.

When the *śāstra* says that knowledge alone is *mokṣa*, it does not amount to fanaticism. If I say that the eyes alone see colours, I am not a fanatic. There is fanaticism only when I propagate a belief, a non-verifiable belief, as truth, the only truth, or hold on to one means as true while there are many equally valid options.

When the self is mistaken for a limited being, *saṁsārī*, nothing other that knowledge can save the person. There can be different forms of prayer because prayer is an action, *karma*, and action is always open to choice. There can also be a choice between a life of *sannyāsa* and that of a *karma-yoga*. But there is only one way of correcting the *saṁsāritva*, a life of becoming, of *ātman* and that is by self-knowledge, for which we require a means of knowledge. The *Bṛhadāraṇyakopaniṣad* states that *ātman* has to be known, for which one has to do *śāstra-vicāra*.[15]

Mokṣa by thought-free mind confusion

Confusion also exists in the thinking that self-realisation is the elimination of all thoughts in the mind. The confusion comes from the statement that *ātman* is undivided, *nirvikalpa*. If absence of thought is self-knowledge, everyone is already enlightened, because who has not slept? Even between two thoughts there is absence of thought. If absence of thought for one split-second is not enlightenment, absence of thought for an hour is not going to make one wiser! It is obvious that absence of thought is not enlightenment. If a thinking person does not know, how will a non-thinking person know? If there is enlightenment in the absence of thought, it will be lost no sooner than a thought occurs; therefore an enlightened person should be permanently without thoughts in order to remain enlightened. It means there will be no enlightened person at all.

The *śāstra* presents the *ātman* as *nirvikalpa*. The vision of the *śāstra* is that while the knower, known and knowledge are not separate from *ātman*, *ātman* is independent of all of them. In the *Māṇḍūkyopaniṣad*, as well as in the *kārikā*, an exposition of the original, the dreamer is cited as a proof that there is no real division, *vikalpa*, such as dreamer, dream and dreamt, even though during the dream the division was taken to be real. The purpose of the dream example is to make us see that the waker's experience of duality is not any different. While the difference between the waker and the dreamer is accepted in terms of qualities, *viśeṣas*, the basic non-difference is shown in detail in the *kārikā*.

In the *jyotir brāhmaṇā* of the *Bṛhadāraṇyakopaniṣad*, the invariable *ātman* in dream and waking is presented as the light of consciousness, *jyotis-svarūpaḥ*. The *svarūpa* of the *ātman* is not the dreamer, dream or dreamt; nor the waker, waking experience or waker's objects. But the knower, known and the knowledge *vikalpa* is also non-separate from the *ātman* and therefore the division is *mithyā*. It is obvious that *ātman* is always *nirvikalpa*, in spite of the apparent division. This is said in the *Kenopaniṣad*, 'in every form of knowledge *ātman* is understood by the discriminative as the invariable.'[16] Therefore, the knowledge that I am thought free, *nirvikalpa*, is in spite of the experience of *vikalpa*. It is entirely different from a state wherein there is absence of thoughts.

In the *aṣṭāṅga yoga*, the *aṅgī,* the main thing to be achieved is *nirvikalpa samādhi,* a state wherein there is the absence of subject-object relationship. Even though it is a desirable accomplishment the state itself should not be construed as self-knowledge. When the mind is in a state of absorption or with thoughts, what obtains as invariable is the *svarūpa* of *ātman,* which is *nirvikalpa.* Again the notion that when there is no more thought then there is enlightenment, implies a duality such as *ātman* and thought. When thought is, *ātman* is not. When *ātman* is, thought is not. Both become equally real because one exists in the absence of the other. This is not true. If one exists whether the other exists, both the objects enjoy the same order of reality, like the table and chair. If one exists only in the absence of the other, they also belong to the same order of reality, like illness and health. Both are equally real.

Does thought deny *ātman?* Is there a thinker without *ātman*? Is there a thought without *ātman*? In fact, thought is *ātman.* But *ātman* is not just a thought. *Ātman* is *satya,* being present in all situations, while situations are *mithyā,* dependent as they are for their existence upon *ātman.* There is no *mithyā* without *adhiṣṭhāna.* The definition of *mithyā* is *adhiṣṭhāna ananyat,* that which is non-separate from its cause.

The wave being not independent of water, you need not remove the wave in order to see the water. So too, if the thinker, the thought and what is thought of, are dependent upon the *ātman,* which is *satya,* you do not have to remove any of them to recognise the *ātman.* The recognition is that all three are *ātman* while *ātman* is not any of them.

Vāsanā-kṣaya confusion

There is a concept that the *ātman* has become the *jīva* due to *vāsanā*s, past impressions. The *vāsanā*s, often equated to *karma-phala,* results of action, like *puṇya* and *pāpa,* are assumed to have been gathered by the *jīva* who has no beginning. The exhaustion of *vāsanā*s through any of the four *yoga*s amounts to self-realisation. The self-realised person who has no more *vāsanā*s to perpetuate his life may continue to exist as a free person, *jīvanmukta,* due to others' *vāsanā*s! The problems caused by this modern *prakriyā* are numerous.

If *vāsanā*s cause the *ātman* to become a *jīva, vāsanā*s become a parallel reality to *ātman.* Then *ātman* ceases to be non-dual and anyone who takes it as non-dual will suffer from an error. If *vāsanā*s are not an independent reality, then they are *mithyā,* depending as they do for their existence upon *ātman.* What is *mithyā* has to be understood as *mithyā.*

Mithyā does not pose any problem if it is understood as such and therefore exhaustion of *vāsanā*s is not necessary. Nor is it possible for any one in a given birth to exhaust all the *vāsanā*s collected in an infinite number of births. In fact, they can be exhausted only in an infinite number of incarnations. So *vāsanā*-exhaustion itself is a dream. Even if the impossible *vāsanā*-exhaustion were achieved, the possibility of a *jīvan-mukta* is nil. When all the *vāsanā*s are exhausted the *jīva* ceases to be. What is left out is *ātman* who is *asaṅgaḥ,* who is unaffected by and unconnected to anything. There is no way the *asaṅga-ātman* will attract anything from *samaṣṭi prārabdha*. If a nucleus, *jīva*, exists, then there are *vāsanā*s to exhaust.

The *śāstra* mentions *vāsanā* exhaustion, but it is purely with reference to the preparedness of the mind, *antaḥ-karaṇa-śuddhi*. The *vāsanā*s that the later *ācārya*s talk about are *viṣaya-vāsanā*, *deha-vāsanā*, and *śāstra-vāsanā*. The fascination for an object, *viṣaya*, thinking that it can give you security and happiness, is a superimposition called *śobhana-adhyāsa*. By *vicāra* you have to remove this superimposition to become the *adhikārī* for self-knowledge. So too, 'I am this body,' *vāsanā* has to be removed by inquiry and contemplation. A craving for the study of *śāstra*s other than Vedanta, *śāstra-vāsanā*, can divert you in the pursuit of self-knowledge. You have to tackle this craving by commitment to *vedānta-vicāra*.

This three-fold *vāsanā* is not presented by *ācārya*s as a cause for the *ātman* to become a *jīva*. The truth to be emphasised here is that *ātman* has never become a *jīva*. *Jīvatva*, the notion of individuality, is a superimposition upon *ātman* due to ignorance. The pursuit is, therefore, to understand that the *svarūpa* of *ātman* is free from *jīvatva*.

Confusion regarding karma-yoga

There is a great deal of confusion about *karma-yoga*. One definition of *karma-yoga* is, 'perform action without expecting results.' Another view, '*karma-yoga* is doing selfless service.' Yet another definition of *karma-yoga* is, 'skill in action.' In fact the most misunderstood topic is *karma-yoga*. The *varṇāśrama-dharma* is nothing but *karma-yoga*. When one performs *nitya-naimittika karma* for the sake of *antaḥ-karaṇa-śuddhi*, it is considered *karma-yoga*, if the person is a *mumukṣu*. Whereas, the person who is interested in *dharma*, *artha* and *kāma* and for that purpose performs the same prayers or rituals is not a *karma yogī*.

No one can perform action without expecting a result, nor can a person skilful in action necessarily be considered a *karma-yogī*. There are many people given to crime who are skilful. The notion that serving a cause is *karma-yoga* is also not totally true, because the cause may be nothing but an expression of a group ego which is as false as one's own small ego. When one's likes and dislikes, *rāga- dveṣas*, subserve *dharma,* then one performs one's duties. That person is not carried away by likes and dislikes, going against *dharma*. Fulfilling one's likes and dislikes at the cost of *dharma* is called attachment to the fruits of action, *phalāśakti*. As long as one performs an action in keeping with *dharma,* whether one likes the action or not, one is a *karma-yogī*.[17]

Karma-yoga is clearly unfolded throughout the *Bhagavad Gītā*. Even if one performs action for the sake of fulfilling one's own likes and dislikes, as long as it is not against the *sāmānya dharma,* universal values, one can still be a *karma-yogī* if one takes the result of action as *prasāda,* coming from the Lord. This attitude is present in the lives of Hindus even today. Building a house is fulfilling a *rāga*. One can build a house without going against *dharma*. But still, the house that is the *karma-phala,* can be offered to the Lord at the time of *gṛhapraveśa* and then it can be taken as *prasāda*. If that attitude is genuine and it is maintained throughout one's life with reference to all achievements, one is a *karma-yogī,* if one has chosen *mokṣa* as his prime goal. A life of *karma-yoga,* which is a *yoga* of attitude with reference to action and its results, will free one from the hold of *rāga-dveṣa*s. One thus becomes ready for self-knowledge as well as *niṣṭhā* there in.

Value preaching

While no one is ignorant of values, values are seldom properly understood. By common sense every human being knows what is universally right and wrong. The problem is in one's understanding of the value of values. If one has understood the value of any value, one will not compromise it for anything—money, power and so on because one knows the enormity of the loss. In fact, for such a person any compromise is a bad bargain. Therefore, a teacher need not preach values but should help the student discover the value of values. Here again there is a process of unfolding involved.

Too many words

As a student when one goes to a teacher to know about the *ātman*, one is told *ātman* is eternal, *nitya*. Here is a typical problem in communication. A teacher can communicate only by words, which are known to him or her as well as to the student. The word, eternal sounds like a known word and therefore the student thinks that he knows the *ātman* but has no experience of the eternal! In fact, the student does not know. All the student knows is that which is non-eternal. Eternal is unlike anything one knows. All that is there with the student is a new word whose meaning has not been unfolded.

The whole teaching is to make the student understand what is eternity. In fact, the word eternal should mean that *ātman* is not non-eternal; *ātman* is timelessness. By inquiry, the one who is aware of time is revealed to be that very consciousness, wherein the concept of time resolves. This consciousness, which is the *svarūpa* of time, is in terms of time called eternity. Similarly every word that talks about *ātman* is to be unfolded by the teacher without leaving any misconception in the student's mind. Even the meaning of consciousness has to be unfolded. When one hears the word apple one is aware of its meaning. However, when one hears the word consciousness, the meaning of the word consciousness does not become an object of consciousness; it is oneself. The teacher must be conscious of all this while unfolding these words. A proper teacher knows how to handle these words because he or she has the clarity in the vision of Vedanta.

In the light of all these, we need to be clear that:

1. Vedanta is an independent means of knowledge,
2. The *prakriyās* must be handled as they are—only as *prakriyās*, and
3. Self-knowledge is not another state of experience; it is the correction of an error about oneself, and the recognition of the invariable self as the truth and basis of all experiences.

Oṁ tat sat

NOTES

1 *nāsti akṛtaḥ kṛtena* (1.2.12)

2 *sadeva saumya idamagra āsīt* (*Chāndogyopaniṣad* 6.2.1)

3 *tadvijñānārthaṁ sa gurumevābhigacchet samitpāṇiḥ śrotriyaṁ brahmaniṣṭham* (*Muṇḍakopaniṣad* 1.2.12)

4 *yanmanasā na manute yenārhumano matam. Tadeva brahma tvaṁ viddhi* (*Kenopaniṣad* 1.2.12)

5 *śāstrayonitvāt* (*Brahmasūtra* 1.1.3)

6 *yato vā imāni bhūtāni jāyante. Yena jātāni jīvanti. Yatprayatyabhisaṁ-viśanti. Tad vijijñāsasva. Tad brahemti.* (*Taittirīyopaniṣad* 3.1.1)

7 *vācārambhaṇaṁ vikāro nāmadheyaṁ mṛttiketyeva satyam.* (*Chāndogyopaniṣad* 6.1.4)

8 *tarati śokamātmavit* (*Chāndogyopaniṣad* 7.1.3)

9 To arrive at the nature of relationship and the degree of reality enjoyed by different objects, this reasoning is employed. One is, the other is: this is *anvaya*. One is not, the other is not: this is *vyatireka*. The existence of a table does not imply the existence of a chair. If it does, then where the table is, the chair is. Where the table is not, the chair is not, which is not true. But if the table is wooden, where the table is, wood is.

Even if the table is broken, still the wood is. By this reasoning we understand that while the existence of a wooden table is dependent upon wood, the wood can exist without being a table. Hence we see the wood has a greater degree of reality than the table. This method is employed in cause-effect analysis, which we saw before.

10 Arundhatī is a star which is close to Vaṣiṣṭha in the *sapta-ṛṣi* configuration of stars and is very small to the naked eye. After the marriage ceremony, a Hindu couple is supposed to see both Vaṣiṣṭha and Arundhatī the *ṛṣi* couple who, acording to the Purāṇās, have imortalised themselves in the form of stars. Having spotted the *sapta-ṛṣi* group one can identify the Vaṣiṣṭha and with some keen observation can eventually see Arundhatī. To lead a person to the sight of Vaṣiṣṭha and Arundhatī in the open sky at night, an adept will use an easily spottable heavenly body as a starting point and lead the person through a visual path to *sapta-ṛṣi* and then to Vaṣiṣṭha. Once Vaṣiṣṭha, which itself is small but visible, is recognised then Arundhatī can be seen. Other than Arundhatī, everything that has been pointed out in the process of recognition is negated. This is *sthūlārundhatī nyāya*. (Modern astronomy says that both Vaṣiṣṭha and

Arundhatī are one star, which appears as two; our forefathers also said they are one even though they appear to be different.)

11 *sa vā eḥa puruṣo'nnarasamayaḥ* (*Taittirīyopaniṣad* 2.1.1)

12 *deśakālavastu aparicchinnam anantam*

13 *nitya aparokṣasya ātmanaḥ jñānam aparokṣameva na tu parokṣam*

14 *sannyāsastu mahābāho duḥkhamāptumayogataḥ* (*Bhagavad Gītā* 5.6)

15 *ātmā vā are draṣṭavyaḥ śrotavyo mantavyo nididhyāsitavyaḥ* (*Bṛhadāraṇyakopaniṣad* 2.4.5)

16 *pratibodhaviditaṁ matam, bodhaṁ bodhaṁ prati viditam* (*Kenopaniṣad* 2.4)

17 *dharmyāddhi yuddhat śreyo'nyat kṣatriyasya na vidyate* (*Bhagavad Gītā* 2.31)

Books by Swami Dayananda Saraswati

Public Talk Series :

1. Living Intelligently
2. Successful Living
3. Need for Cognitive Change
4. Discovering Love
5. The Value of Values
6. Vedic View and Way of Life

Upaniṣad Series :

7. Muṇḍakopaniṣad
8. Kenopaniṣad

Prakaraṇa Series :

9. Tattvabodhaḥ

Text Translation Series :

10. Śrīmad Bhagavad Gītā
 (Text with roman transliteration and English translation)
11. Śrī Rudram
 (Text in Sanskrit with transliteration, word-to-word and verse meaning along with an elaborate commentary in English)

Stotra Series :

12. Dīpārādhanā
13. Prayer Guide
    (With explanations of several Mantras, Stotras, Kirtans and Religious Festivals)

Moments with Oneself Series :

14. Freedom from Helplessness
15. Living versus Getting On
16. Insights
17. Action and Reaction
18. Fundamental Problem
19. Problem is You, Solution is You
20. Purpose of Prayer
21. Vedanta 24x7
22. Freedom
23. Crisis Management
24. Surrender and Freedom
25. The Need for Personal Reorganisation
26. Freedom in Relationship
27. Stress-free Living
28. Om Namo Bhagavate Vāsudevāya
29. Yoga of Objectivity
30. Īśvara in One's Life

Bhagavad Gītā

31. Bhagavad Gītā Home Study Course (Hardbound - 9 Volumes)

Meditation Series :

32. Morning Meditation Prayers
33. What is Meditation?

Essays :

34. Do all Religions have the same goal?
35. Conversion is Violence
36. Gurupūrṇimā
37. Dānam
38. Japa
39. Can We?
40. Moments with Krishna
41. Teaching Tradition of Advaita Vedanta
42. Compositions of Swami Dayananda Saraswati

Exploring Vedanta Series : (*vākyavicāra*)

43. śraddhā bhakti dhyāna yogād avaihi ātmānaṁ ced vijānīyāt

Books translated in other languages and in English based on Swami Dayananda Saraswati's Original Exposition

Tamil

44. Veeduthorum Gitopadesam (9 Volumes)
    (Bhagavad Gītā Home Study Course)
45. Dānam

Kannada

46. Mane maneyalli Adhyayana (7 Volumes)
    (Bhagavad Gītā Home Study Course)
47. Vedanta Pravesike

Malayalam

48. Muṇḍakopaniṣad

Telugu

49. Kenopaniṣad

Hindi

50. Ghar baithe Gītā Vivechan (Vol 1)
    (Bhagavad Gītā Home Study Course)
51. Antardṛṣṭi (Insights)
52. Vedanta 24X7
53. Kriya aur Pratikriya (Action and Reaction)

Marathi

54. Gruhe Gītā Adhyayan (Vol 1 available)
    (Bhagavad Gītā Home Study Course)

English

55. The Jungian Myth and Advaita Vedanta
56. The Vedantic Self and the Jungian Psyche
57. Salutations to Rudra
58. Without a Second

Biography (Hardbound Deluxe)

59. Swami Dayananda Saraswati
Contributions & Writings
(Smt. Sheela Balaji)

Biography (Hardbound Regular)

60. Swami Dayananda Saraswati
Contributions & Writings
(Smt. Sheela Balaji)

Also available at :

ARSHA VIDYA RESEARCH
AND PUBLICATION TRUST
32 / 4 Sir Desika Road
Mylapore Chennai 600 004
Telefax : 044 - 2499 7131
Email : avrandpt@gmail.com
Website : www.avrpt.com

ARSHA VIDYA GURUKULAM
Anaikatti P.O.
Coimbatore 641 108
Ph : 0422 - 2657001
Fax : 0422 - 2657002
Email : office@arshavidya.in
Website : www.arshavidya.in

ARSHA VIDYA GURUKULAM
P.O.Box 1059. Pennsylvania
PA 18353, USA
Ph : 001 -570 -992 -2339
Email : avp@epix.net
Website : www.arshavidya.org

SWAMI DAYANANDA ASHRAM
Purani Jhadi, P.B.No. 30
Rishikesh, Uttaranchal 249 201
Telefax : 0135 - 2430769
Email : ashrambookstore@yahoo.com
Website : www.dayananda.org

Other leading Book Stores:

Chennai:	**044**
Motilal Banarsidass	2498 2315
Giri Trading	2495 1966
Higginbothams	2851 3519
Pustak Bharati	2461 1345
Theosophical Publishing House	2446 6613 / 2491 1338
The Odessey	43910300
Bengaluru:	**080**
Gangarams	2558 1617 / 2558 1618
Sapna Book House	4011 4455 / 4045 5999
Strand Bookstall	2558 2222, 2558 0000
Vedanta Book House	2650 7590
Coimbatore:	**0422**
Guru Smruti	9486773793
Giri Trading	2541523
New Delhi:	**011**
Motilal Banarsidass	2385 8335 / 2385 1985
Trivandrum:	**0471**
Prabhus Bookhouse	2478397 / 2473496

Kozhikode:	**0495**
Ganga Bookhouse	6521262
Mumbai:	**022**
Chetana Bookhouse	2285 1243 / 2285 3412
Strand Bookstall	2266 1994 / 2266 1719/
	2261 4613
Giri Trading	2414 3140
Bardoli (Surat):	**0622**
Dr. Anil Patwardhan	220283
(BGHS course - Marathi)	0-9377715684
Mysore :	
Swamini Varadananda	0-9242890144
(BGHS course - Kannada)	0-8762464014